DYNAMIC STUDIES IN GALATIANS

BRINGING GOD'S WORD TO LIFE

FRED A. SCHEEREN

WESTBOW
PRESS
A DIVISION OF THOMAS NELSON
& ZONDERVAN

Scripture references marked NLT are taken from the Holy Bible, New Living Translation, copyright 1996. Used by permission of Tyndale House Publishers, Inc., Wheaton, Illinois 60189. All rights reserved.

Scripture references marked KJV are taken from the King James Version of the Bible.

Scripture references marked NASB are taken from the New American Standard Bible, © 1960, 1963, 1968, 1971, 1972, 1973, 1975, 1977 by The Lockman Foundation. Used by permission.

Scripture references marked AMP are taken from the Amplified® Bible, Copyright © 1954, 1958, 1962, 1964, 1965, 1987 by The Lockman Foundation. Used by permission. (www.Lockman.org)

WestBow Press books may be ordered through booksellers or by contacting:

WestBow Press
A Division of Thomas Nelson & Zondervan
1663 Liberty Drive
Bloomington, IN 47403
www.westbowpress.com
1 (866) 928-1240

Because of the dynamic nature of the Internet, any web addresses or links contained in this book may have changed since publication and may no longer be valid. The views expressed in this work are solely those of the author and do not necessarily reflect the views of the publisher, and the publisher hereby disclaims any responsibility for them.

Any people depicted in stock imagery provided by Thinkstock are models, and such images are being used for illustrative purposes only. Certain stock imagery © Thinkstock.

ISBN: 978-1-4908-4333-9 (sc)
ISBN: 978-1-4908-4334-6 (e)

Library of Congress Control Number: 2014912220

Printed in the United States of America.

WestBow Press rev. date: 07/10/2014

DEDICATION

I DEDICATE THIS book to my lovely wife, Sally, who is a Jewish believer. She has stood by me over the years and raised our sons in our God-loving home. The comfort of sharing our friendship and our love for Christ has encouraged me greatly in creating this series of dynamic studies of various books of the Bible. Sally's participation in our small group studies has added a much deeper dimension of richness to the discussions. Thank you for sharing your heritage, training, and knowledge.

CONTENTS

Acknowledgments ix

Preface xi

Introduction: Ground Rules...xiii

Background to the Book of Galatians............................. xv

Week 1: The Battle Begins (Galatians 1:1-10) 1

Week 2: God's Call Upon Paul and God's Call Upon You
         (Galatians 1:11-24) 9

Week 3: One Body, One Spirit, One Hope (Galatians 2:1-10) 17

Week 4: Eternal Vigilance: The Price of Freedom (Galatians 2:11-21)........... 25

Week 5: From Bewitched to Grafted by Faith (Galatians 3:1-14) 33

Week 6: The Law, the Promise, and Faith (Galatians 3:15-25) 43

Week 7: True Children of God (Galatians 3:26-4:7)..................................... 51

Week 8: Staying on the Road of Truth (Galatians 4:8-20) 63

Week 9: Freedom in Christ (Galatians 4:21-31) 71

Week 10: Fight to Stay Free (Galatians 5:1-15) 81

Week 11: Fruit of the Holy Spirit (Galatians 5:16-26) 93

Week 12: Doing Good to Everyone (Galatians 6:1-10).............................. 107

Week 13: What Really Matters (Galatians 6:11-18)......................................117

Appendix 1: How to Avoid Error... 127

ACKNOWLEDGMENTS

MY FRIEND, BOB Mason, who at the time I prepared this material was in his second career as the pastor of small groups at the Bible Chapel in the South Hills of Pittsburgh, suggested the overall structure of each study. Realizing our group was doing more in-depth work than most, he asked that I include several important segments in each lesson—most specifically, the warm-up and life application phases.

Bob suggested a great resource called the *New Testament Lesson Planner* from InterVarsity Press. I have augmented this with commentaries by Chuck Missler from Koinonia House, the *Wiersbe Bible Commentary*, and the whole of Scripture itself. To make the utilization of the whole of Scripture more efficient, I have also leaned heavily on the Libronix Digital Library, perhaps the most advanced Bible software available, and other resources to help us understand how the New Testament and the Tanakh (Old Testament) fit together as one cohesive document.

I have also enjoyed the input and encouragement of my friend, Ron Jones, as I have continued to prepare these studies. Ron is a former high school principal and administrator. He is also a committed believer and daily student of God's Word. His background in education coupled with his love of God and His Word has made him a powerful force for good. It has been my privilege to work with him in presenting material from the Dynamic Bible Studies series to our ABF (Adult Bible Fellowship) group, also at the Bible Chapel.

In addition, it has been my privilege to discuss many of the Jewish customs and practices of the time when this book was written with my friend, Rabbi Jeff Kipp. Rabbi Kipp is outstanding among Jewish Rabbis in that he has realized that Jesus of Nazareth is indeed Yeshua Ha-Maschiach, the Jewish Messiah. Be able to discuss and review certain points of the text, customs and practices involved has been an invaluable resource.

For the first time in the course of preparing the studies that make up the Dynamic Bible Studies series I had at my disposal a gift from one of the members of the small group Bible study of which I am privileged to be a part. Joyce Fink, one of our members, served as the assistant to the president at Pittsburgh Theological Seminary. Her first husband, Bill, was a respected Bible teacher prior to his death from pancreatic cancer. His life, and the manner in which he faced death, was a great witness to those with whom he came into contact. Joyce honored me with the gift of Bill's favorite resource—a printed edition of the vaunted Matthew Henry commentaries. I was humbled, touched, and grateful for her gift and am appreciative of the contributions she brings to our group.

Speaking of small groups, Dr. Chuck Missler, a former Fortune 500 CEO, said "I experienced more growth in my personal life as a believer by participating in small group bible studies than anything else." I believe you may find this to be true in your experience and encourage you to be an active participant in such a mutually supportive, biblically-based group.

May God bless you, inspire you, teach you, and change your life for the better as you work through these lessons.

PREFACE

WELCOME TO WHAT I hope you will find to be a most enjoyable study of the book of Galatians, part of the Judeo-Christian document which we have come to know as the Bible. Many believers claim Galatians as one of their favorite portions of Scripture because of its powerful message about the grace of God and the true freedom a believer has available through Jesus Christ. When studied with the book of James, we come away with innumerable practical applications to a vital and victorious everyday life.

As we consider how this book fits into the whole of the New Testament and the Tanakh (the name used by Jews for the Old Testament, used here to emphasize the Jewishness of the Scriptures), we need to realize a number of things. We should stand in awe of this collection of 66 books, written over thousands of years by at least 40 different authors. Every detail of the text is there by design. It explains history before it happens, and comes to us from outside the dimension of time. It is, in short, the most amazing, most authenticated, and most accurate book available in the world.

If this claim is not strong enough, add to it the indisputable fact that the words contained therein have changed more lives than any others now in existence.

And now back to this particular study.

I intended this particular study to be used in a small group setting, however, it can also be adapted to a larger group or individual study.

While the Judeo-Christian Scriptures are demonstrably perfect, my prepared studies are not. There is no way I or anyone else could possibly incorporate the depth of the text into individual sessions. I simply desire to provide a vehicle for others to use in their investigation of the Scriptures as they incorporate these timeless truths into their lives.

One perfect example of the depth of the Scriptures and the impossibility of capturing that depth all at one time comes from an interesting experience I had when putting together similar lessons on the book of Romans. One Saturday morning, I wrote three lessons in one sitting. By the time I finished the third, I was mentally exhausted. About a month later, when it came time to present the third lesson, I forgot I had already prepared it. I spent two more hours writing the study again. When I realized my mistake, I compared the two and was surprised to find how different they were. Every time we plumb the depths of God's Word, we are sure to find more than we have ever seen. I hope this excites you as much as it does me.

INTRODUCTION
GROUND RULES

I DESIGNED THE first portion of each study to encourage readers to think about their personal situation. I designed the second portion to help people understand what the text says and how it relates to the whole of Scripture. And finally, each lesson ends with a discussion designed to help people apply that lesson.

You will notice that, in most instances, I have included the citation, but not the actual text of the Scripture we are considering. I did this on purpose. I believe we all learn more effectively if we have to dig out the text itself. As a byproduct of that exercise, we become more familiar with this marvelous book.

Scripture references are preceded by or followed by a question or series of questions. Again, I did this on purpose. I have also found that people seem to learn most effectively when employing the Socratic Method. That is, instead of telling someone what the text says and how it relates to other texts and life, they will remember it better if they answer questions about it and ferret out the information for themselves.

In a few instances, I have inserted additional commentary or partial answers to some of the questions to help the group get the most out of the study.

In addition, I added various scriptural references, intending that they be read out loud as part of the session. Shorter passages might be read by one participant, while anything over two or three verses might serve everyone better if one member reads one verse and another reads the next until the passage is completed. This keeps everyone involved. After reading these passages, I intend that how they relate to the primary Scripture at hand in Galatians be seriously considered. At times, this relationship seems to be available and obvious on the surface. In many other instances, the interconnectedness of the whole of Scripture and its principles are most effectively understood through deeper thought, discussion, and prayer.

In commenting on and discussing the various passages, questions, concepts, and principles in this material, it is not required that any particular person give his or her input. The reader of any passage may, but is not pressured to, give his or her thoughts to the group. This is a group participation exercise for the mutual benefit of all involved and many people in the group giving their insight into a certain verse or question will often enhance the learning experience.

I also have two practical suggestions if you work through this book in a small group setting. Every time you meet, I suggest you review the calendar and agree upon the next scheduled meeting as well as who will bring refreshments. This will help the group to run a lot more smoothly while enhancing everyone's enjoyment and expectations.

BACKGROUND TO THE BOOK OF GALATIANS

THERE ARE TWENTY-SEVEN books in the New Testament, over half of which were written through one man: Saul of Tarsus, aka Paul.

The book of Galatians is regarded by many as one of Paul's greatest and most important letters.

Dr. Merrill Tenney, writing in *Galatians: The Charter of Christian Liberty* speaks about the importance of this epistle:

> Few books have had a more profound influence on the history of mankind than this small tract, for such it should be called. Christianity might have been just one more Jewish sect, and the thought of the Western world might have been entirely pagan had it never been written. Galatians embodies the germinal teaching on Christian freedom which separated Christianity from Judaism, and which launched it upon a career of missionary conquest. It was the cornerstone of the Protestant Reformation, because its teaching of salvation by grace alone became the dominant theme of the preaching of the Reformers.

Paul's conversion is perhaps most effectively referenced in Galatians 1:11-17. As a result of his new life in Christ, his former friends became his fiercest enemies and tried to kill him.

In the book of Galatians, Paul addresses the problem with the Judaizers. These legalists gained their moniker from the Latin word *Judaizo*, which means "to be or live like a Jew." The term is a religious designation and has nothing to do with nationality. These Judaizers were opponents of early Christian missionaries. This may be surprising since the Judaizers were themselves believers in Yeshua Ha-Maschiah, Jesus Christ, the Jewish Messiah.

Prior to the coming of Christ, if a person wanted to become godly, he or she converted to Judaism and began to follow Jewish ceremonial laws. Even after Jesus was born, murdered, and rose from the dead, the Judaizers erroneously believed one must first convert to Judaism.

In the minds of the Judaizers, the Gentiles represented corruption—false gods, drunkenness, fornication, dishonesty, hatred, conflict, arrogance, evil, unfaithfulness, violence, and foolish impulsiveness. In their minds, one had to first leave these practices behind and turn toward the "good" practices found in Judaism.

However, God made it clear to them, through Paul, that the good news of Jesus Christ was not an addendum to Judaism. Instead, it was the end and fulfillment of the Law. Through the gospel of Christ, the grace of God would extend beyond Israel and beyond the Jewish religion and race. Blind to this truth, the Judaizers replaced the heart of Christianity with one of stone: legalism. God used Paul to not only oppose this fallacy, but to expound upon the truth of the gospel and the joy and freedom that goes with it.

As you begin to read the book of Galatians, you can immediately see that something is very wrong in this particular church. False teachers are spreading a false gospel and Paul is engaging them in a battle for the vitality, veracity, and freedom of the faith.

In some ways the book of Galatians is best studied as part of a trilogy. This trilogy relates specifically to one very important verse from the Old Testament, which Jewish scholars call the Tanakh. In particular we should take a look at Habakkuk 2:4 which says:

"Look at the proud! They trust in themselves, and their lives are crooked; but the righteous will live by their faith." (NLT)

"Behold the proud, His soul is not upright in him; But the just shall live by his faith." (KJV)

This quote from Habakkuk could be said to tie directly into the New Testament books of Romans, Galatians, and Hebrews.

Romans tell us who is considered just or righteous.

Galatians tells us how they shall live.

Hebrews teaches us about the faith and obedience of these people.

With this perspective, one can gain a deeper appreciation of the book of Galatians. By reading it together with the New Testament books of Hebrews and Romans we gain a better understanding about how a follower of God should live.

THE BATTLE BEGINS
GALATIANS 1:1-10

Opening Prayer

Group Warm-up Question

How would you start a letter to a loved one if you had something difficult to share that required a change in their behavior?

Read: Galatians 1:1-10
Reread: Galatians 1:1-3

How did Paul identify himself as he opened his letter?

Who joined Paul in sending this letter to the Galatians?

Why was Paul's position as an apostle so unique and important?

Read: Acts 26:15-18 and comment.

After identifying his position in Galatians 1:1, why does Paul transition directly to the subject of the resurrection?

Read: 1 Corinthians 15 and comment.

Reread: Galatians 1:3

The word "grace" in Greek appears as *charis,* and in the sense of the New Testament means "unmerited favor." The word Paul uses for "peace" is *shalom*, a Hebrew greeting and wish for personal peace.

How does experiencing the grace of God enable one to then experience the peace of God?

Reread: Galatians 1: 4

How did Paul describe the work of Jesus Christ in this verse?

Read the following verses to see the masterful way in which this was summarized in…..

Galatians 1:4

Psalm 49:7-8

Matthew 20:28

2 Corinthians 5:21

Galatians 3:13

Isaiah 53:10

How did Paul speak of the purpose of God's grace toward us in Galatians 1:4?

How did he describe the source of this grace?

Reread: Galatians 1:5

How does this verse help us understand the reason for God's grace?

Read the following verses for additional insight into the purpose, workings, and result of God's grace toward us:

2 Timothy 1:9

1 Samuel 2:6-9

Romans 11:6

Setting the Stage

At this point we should stop and examine the way God prepared the Galatians for the content of this serious letter. Paul goes through the following steps:

1. He establishes his special and unique authority.
2. He establishes the power of the One who gave him this authority.
3. He establishes and reminds his readers of the vital importance of the resurrection of Christ and of the privilege they have to experience the same thing.
4. He establishes the fact that no human deserves God's grace.
5. He establishes that one can only experience true inner peace through God's grace.
6. He establishes, in short form, the tremendous work of Jesus Christ.
7. He reminds readers of the reason God extended His grace to them.

Why do you think Paul began this letter this way?

Some scholars would say that this progression works perfectly to set up a backdrop for an effective attack on the problem being experienced by the Galatians.

The Problem

Read: Galatians 1:6-7

In short, what was the serious problem plaguing the Galatians?

In particular, these early believers were being tempted to discard God's grace in favor of their own legalistic system of works. Why are human beings today still so vulnerable to the temptation to rely on themselves instead of God's grace?

Reread: Galatians 1: 7

The church in Galatia was being influenced by another gospel. In the Greek there are two words that might be used for "another." One word is *heteron*, which means another that is different. The other is *allo*, which is another that is of the same kind. The word Paul used in Galatians 1:7 is *heteron*, which indicates that it is a completely different gospel that is wholly unlike the gospel of Christ.

What is the importance of this distinction?

The Greek word used for "pervert" in Galatians 1: 7 is *metastrepho*, which means to twist, distort, to turn about, to change into an opposite character and also points to clever deceivers, enchanters and bewitchers.

Read: Galatians 3:1 to see Paul's direct application of this concept.

The Greek word translated "pervert or distort" is used only three times in the New Testament. In each case we can clearly see that it means to change something to the opposite of its original intention.

This can be observed in each of the following three verses:

Acts 2:20

Galatians 1:7

James 4:9

Reread: Galatians 1:8-9

What did Paul say about those who would distort the purity of the gospel?

Why did Paul react so vehemently to these people?

How is one treating the grace of God if the good news of Christ is distorted?

Read: Galatians 2:21 and answer.

Question: How does God Himself feel about those who distort His Word?

Reread Galatians 1:9 and also read Revelation 22:18-19 in thinking about your answer.

Reread: Galatians 1:10

Here we see that the adversaries of the gospel were personally attacking Paul.

It is possible that they were twisting his statement found in 1 Corinthians 9:22.

We can also see Paul's personal motivation in 2 Corinthians 5:9.

Conversely we see the true motivation of those he is opposing in Galatians 4:17.

This is an interesting example of the psychological term "transference" whereby someone, sometimes unconsciously, attributes his or her own attitudes, thought patterns, behaviors, and aggressions to a third party when that person believes he or she is being opposed by the party in question. We can see this concept at work in our world today, when we are aware of it. A politician caught in a lie may respond by saying his opponent is lying. A person who encourages someone who is upset to calm down, may be accused by the person he or she is trying to help as being the one who is upset.

The Judaizers seem to have been accusing Paul of acting from some of the same negative motives they have as they engage in the process of transference.

Read Galatians 1:10 again to see Paul's attitude about pleasing men and God. This was his consistent attitude after he came to know Jesus Christ in a personal way.

Application Question

How can you prepare to respond appropriately and effectively the next time you hear a distorted message or statement about Christ?

Close in Prayer

GOD'S CALL UPON PAUL AND GOD'S CALL UPON YOU
GALATIANS 1:11-24

Opening Prayer

Group Warm-Up Question

What personal accomplishment, achievement, or award are you most proud of?

Read: Galatians 1:11-24

Reread: Galatians 1:11-12

How did Paul first come to learn about and accept the good news of Jesus Christ?

To expand upon this, read Acts: 9:1-22

What did Paul learn from this initial experience? Make a list.

Read 1 Corinthians 15:1-11 to see, in short, what comprised the good news that Paul was privileged to preach. List the basic components of this message below:

1.

2.

3.

4.

5.

6.

7.

Reread: Galatians 1:13

For an expanded view of what we learned in Galatians 1:13, read these verses:

Acts 8:1

Acts 3

Acts 9:1

Acts 22:4-5

Acts 26:9-11

1 Corinthians 15:9

Philippians 3:6

1 Timothy 1:13

Exactly what did Paul do to try and exterminate the early believers? Please list as many things as you can.

Read: Acts 9:26-28

How did Paul's earlier attempts to destroy the first believers impact his relationship with the believers in Jerusalem when he became a believer himself?

How do you think you would have responded to Paul if you had been part of the early church?

How do you respond today when you see God changing someone like he changed Paul?

We should also realize that Paul was:

1. An adherent of Judaism beyond repute

2. A brilliant scholar

3. An influential Jewish leader

4. A zealous opponent of all faiths alien to Judaism

5. A student of the most brilliant and respected Jewish teacher of the time

6. The most respected and promising young Jewish rabbi of his day

7. Perhaps the most intelligent, well educated man of his time

Read the following references to gain an understanding of Paul's unique qualifications:

Galatians 1:14

Acts 26: 5

Acts 5:34

Acts 22:3

Acts 26:24

Reread: Galatians 1:15-16

God did three specific things for Paul that are mentioned in these verses. What were they?

1.

2.

3.

In what ways does God do similar things for believers today?

Reread: Galatians 1:16-19

When Paul became a follower of Jesus Christ, what resources did he have that helped him grow as a believer?

How did Paul's in-depth command and knowledge of the Tanakh, which we call the Old Testament, help him understand the new covenant in Jesus Christ?

What other important truths did Paul learn firsthand during this time of growth?

Read the following verses and list at least three:

Revelation 4:11

1 John 2:6

I John 4:17

With which other apostles did Paul meet in Jerusalem?

When you first became a believer, what resources, activities, or people helped you grow in your faith?

What helps you grow in your relationship with Christ now?

Reread: Galatians 1:20-24

Where did Paul go to share the good news after his first visit to Jerusalem?

What was Paul's relationship to the believers in Jerusalem and Judea during this period of time?

In the final analysis, how did the churches and believers in Judea respond to what they heard Paul was doing?

How should we respond when we hear about the work God is doing in places far removed from us and our experience?

Application Question

God had a special plan for Paul's life. He also has a special plan for the life of every believer. What is God's plan for your life, so far as you understand it, at this point in your journey through this world?

Close in Prayer

ONE BODY, ONE SPIRIT, ONE HOPE

GALATIANS 2:1-10

Opening Prayer

Group Warm-up Questions

Whose opinion of your work, life, and actions is important to you?

After first answering the above question in relationship to God, then answer it as it relates to human beings. In one sentence describe how the two answers work together.

Read: Acts 15

This background material will help us get more out of Galatians 2:1-10.

Read: Galatians 2:1-10

When Paul went back to Jerusalem, who did he take with him?

Remember that he accompanied Paul on his first missionary journey. What else do we know about Barnabus? Read the following verses and list what we learn about him:

Acts 9:26-28

Acts 11:19-24

Acts 11:25-26

Acts 11: 27-30

1.

2.

3.

4.

5.

6.

7.

It is of some interest to note that the name Barnabus means "son of encouragement." We also find Barnabus involved with the situation that erupted with a young John Mark when he left Paul early on. Read the following verses and discuss them to see this:

Acts 13:13

Acts 15:36-41

Colossians 4:10

2 Timothy 4:11

What was the long term result of Barnabus' encouragement when early divisions and difficulties arose between John Mark and Paul?

What lessons can we draw for our lives from the way Barnabus handled divisions and difficulties?

In addition to Barnabus, Titus also accompanied Paul on the trip back to Jerusalem. Read the following verses and list what we learn about Titus:

Galatians 2:3

Titus 1:4-5

2 Corinthians 7

Why is it significant that Titus was a Gentile from Greece?

How did God use Titus in some of the more difficult situations that arose in the early church?

Reread: Galatians 2:1-2

Why did Paul want the opportunity to meet specifically with the Jewish leaders of the early church in Jerusalem?

Why do you think he wanted to meet with them in private?

Read: Galatians 2:3

How did these leaders respond to Paul?

Read:

Galatians 2: 4-5

Acts 15: 1

What do we learn about the "false brothers" who infiltrated this meeting?

What did these false brothers miss about the meaning of circumcision? Read the following verses and explain:

Deuteronomy 10:16

Jeremiah 4:1-4

Romans 2:25-29

Colossians 2:10-11

Philippians 3:1-3

How did Paul, Barnabus, and Titus respond to these false brothers?

What vital motive did Paul and his compatriots have in responding to these Judaizers as they did?

Read: Acts 11:19

To what group did the other apostles limit their preaching of the good news?

Reread: Galatians 2:6

How did the leaders in Jerusalem respond to what Paul was preaching?

Even though Paul respected the leaders in Jerusalem, he was not impressed by their position or their person. What lesson might we learn from this?

How does what we read in Matthew 10:28 relate to this concept?

Reread: Galatians 2:7-9

How did James, Peter, and John respond to Paul's mission from God?

Some of you may have seen the movie *The Blues Brothers*. The brothers claimed they were on a "mission from God." Many other people in the world today make the same claim. By what standard must we judge any supposed "mission from God?"

Read 1 Timothy 3:16-17 and explain.

How do Psalm 133:1 and Galatians 3:28 relate to Galatians 2:7-9?

Interestingly, a brief summary of the gospel preached by Paul and Peter can be found in:

- 1 Peter 1:18-20 (Peter)

- Acts 13:32-39 (Paul)

There is no difference. One may be a little fuller than the other, but there is no conflict at all in what Paul and Peter said in these verses, or in their other writings. Of course, this should come as no surprise to us since we know that all Scripture operates as an integrated message system as we just saw in 2 Timothy 3:16-17.

Reread: Galatians 2:10

What one request did the leaders in Jerusalem make of Paul, Barnabus, and Titus?

Does the way the question was asked indicate that they were already doing this?

What changes then did the leading believers in Jerusalem ask Paul and his fellow workers to make?

Why must correct doctrine go hand in hand with correct actions and duty?

Read James 2:14-26 and Acts 11:27-30 in formulating your answer.

Application Question

It is obvious from the text under consideration today that God calls people to different duties, ministries, and places. And yet at the same time we are all called to preach the same gospel from the same Scriptures in order to build and encourage the body of believers.

Specifically, how can God use you in the circumstances in which you now find yourself, as part of this ongoing effort?

Close in Prayer

WEEK 4

ETERNAL VIGILANCE: THE PRICE OF FREEDOM
GALATIANS 2:11-21

Opening Prayer

Group Warm-up Questions

When a colleague or friend does something wrong, how do you tend to confront him or her?

How do you typically respond when someone confronts or criticizes you about your words or actions?

Read: Galatians 2:11-21

Reread: Galatians 2:11

What did Paul do when Peter visited Antioch?

Why was it important that he do this publicly?

Reread: Galatians 2:12

What did Peter do when he first arrived in Antioch?

How and why did Peter change his behavior for the worse?

Reread: Galatians 2:13

What impact did Peter's actions have upon the other Jewish believers?

Here we see Peter, Barnabas, and other stalwart believers falling into error. Which believers today are immune from falling into error and needing correction?

Is any human being immune from this?

What do we learn about our own lives and responsibilities when we see the way Peter's actions influenced others?

Reread: Galatians 2:14

What did Paul say first in response to Peter's incorrect behavior?

Reread: Galatians 2:15-16

Also Read:

Romans 3:28

Romans 10:4

Galatians 3:21-22

How is a person justified before God?

Read the following verses and discuss how a believer is able to avoid being a law breaker and live a life that is pleasing to God:

Galatians 2:17-19

Romans 7: 4

Romans 7:6

Romans 6:14

Galatians 2:20

Romans 6: 3-4

Romans 6: 8-11

Romans 8: 2

Note that many of these verses come from the book of Romans. This helps us to see the interconnectedness of all of Scripture and in particular how Romans, Galatians, and Hebrews seem to relate together regarding Habakkuk 2:4, where we read that "the just shall live by faith." This can be seen in the trilogy of these New Testament books as follows:

- Who are the just? (Romans)
- How shall they live? (Galatians)
- How do we understand faith? (Hebrews)

Reread: Galatians 2:20

How did Peter inadvertently and almost unconsciously set aside God's grace?

What important life lesson for all believers do we find in this verse?

Reread: Galatians 2:21

If righteousness were possible by keeping the Law, why would Christ's death on the cross have been useless?

What are we doing in a very real sense if we think we can be saved by merely obeying the Law?

What is the extreme danger in this?

This brings us to an important point in our discussion. Peter's mistake inherently denied five important scriptural truths. He would have been horrified if he realized that this was the result of his actions. Being inconsistent with Scripture has many negative inherent consequences beyond what we may see immediately. Conversely, being consistent with the Word of God has positive consequences and results beyond what may be immediately evident to us.

The Five Scriptural Truths Peter Inadvertently Denied

1. The unity of the body of believers (Galatians 2:14)

2. Justification by faith (Galatians 2:15-16)

3. Freedom from the Law (Galatians 2:17-18)

4. The very gospel itself (Galatians 2:19-20)

5. The Grace of God (Galatians 2:21)

Understanding this might cause a believer to ask several important questions about his or her own life, including:

1. Have I been made right with God by His grace? (Ephesians 2:8-9, Romans 11:6)

2. Am I joyful and peaceful as a result of knowing I am justified by trusting Jesus Christ? (Romans 8:1, Romans 5:1)

3. Am I acting in the positive freedom afforded me by God's grace? (Ephesians 2:10)

4. Am I ready to defend the truth of the gospel despite the pressures of the world? (Galatians 1:10)

5. Am I living according to the truth of God's Word? As Dr. David Fink likes to say, "What you do speaks so loudly that I cannot hear what you say."

Read Galatians 1:6-9 to remind ourselves of the absolute imperativeness of sticking to the truth of God's Word.

Application Questions:

How can you show courage and compassion in resisting well-meaning believers who want to impose their own rules on others?

How can you help these people remain true to the Word of God?

Close in Prayer

FROM BEWITCHED TO GRAFTED BY FAITH
GALATIANS 3:1-14

Opening Prayer

Group Warm-Up Question:

If someone close to you showed a lack of knowledge about an important topic, how could you most effectively help them? What tone would you take while doing so?

Read: Galatians 3:1-14

Reread: Galatians 3:1

Why do you think Paul utilized so severe a tone at the beginning of this passage?

The Greek word translated "evidently set forth" in the KJV is *prographo.* This word encompasses more than we might realize upon an initial reading. The definition includes:

1. To write before (in time); set forth of old or designated beforehand (as in the scriptures of the Old Testament)

2. To depict or portray openly; to write before the eyes of all who can read; to depict, portray, paint, before the eyes

Taking this definition into account, exactly how would you explain the fullness of what Paul meant when he referred to what had previously been learned by the Galatians about the crucifixion of Jesus Christ?

What might have happened to make the Galatians lose their grasp of the truth?

Read: Ephesians 2:8-9

What important concept do we find in these verses?

Paul asks the Galatians four questions to drive home the concept found in Ephesians 2:8-9.

1. Reread Galatians 3:2 and answer Paul's first question about faith. How did you receive the Holy Spirit? Note, as Paul mentioned in Galatians 4:6, he did not question their salvation, but was reminding them about the process.

2. Reread Galatians 3:3 and review Paul's second question: On a personal level, how will you then be sanctified? He seems to be asking why they thought that keeping the Law by their own efforts would aid them as they were perfected.

    It was necessary for Paul to ask this question since the Judaizers were misleading some believers as we see in:

    Galatians 4:10

    Galatians 5:2

    Galatians 6:13

Paul is trying to drive home the point that *the means of justification and sanctification are the same.* In other words:

Means of Justification=Means of Sanctification

or

Means of Being Made Right with God=Means of
Growing and Being Perfected by God

How would you put this concept in your own words?

3. Reread Galatians 3:4 and put Paul's third question in your own words.

Read Acts 14:21-22 and relate this to Galatians 3:4.

Why would the Galatians suffer in vain if they could be made right with God by following the Law on their own?

4. Reread Galatians 3:5

What Does Paul ask the Galatians in this verse and how does he answer it?

Read Acts 14:3 and Acts 14:8-11 and discuss how hearing leads to faith.

Why do human beings often become so attracted to a list of rules to obey with a promised result?

What is an example of this in your own experience?

Give a modern day example of someone with a propensity to create rules who ended up in error.

How do certain groups, and even cults take advantage of this?

Reread: Galatians 3:6-9

Upon what basis was Abraham counted as righteous?

Read: Genesis 15:6 to see this in the Old Testament.

   Abraham's righteousness occurred before he became the first Jew and was circumcised. His circumcision did not occur until Genesis 17:23-24.

If God counted Abraham as righteous prior to his being circumcised, how could the Judaizers legitimately claim that going through this procedure was necessary to be accepted by God?

Who, according to Galatians 3:6-9, are the real "children of Abraham?"

Read: Genesis 12:3 to see God promising to bless all the families on earth through Abraham and his descendants the Jews, via the Jewish Messiah, Jesus Christ. It is important to remember that while Jews and Gentiles can both become spiritual descendants of Abraham, they still retain their identities.

A "true Jew," in the fullest sense, is a Jew who has trusted Jesus Christ (Romans 9:6-9). While Gentiles are privileged to share in this special relationship with God, they are warned to not grow arrogant about it (Romans 11:17-18).

Read: Romans 11:6

How does this coincide with what we just read in Galatians 3:6-9?

Reread: Galatians 3:10

Also read: Deuteronomy 27:26

There are 613 commandments in the Old Testament book of the law. According to these verses, how many of these commandments must be obeyed to be put right with God?

Is this possible?

Reread: Galatians 3:11

Also read: Habakkuk 2:4

According to these verses, what is the only way a just and righteous person may be made right with God and experience life to the fullest?

What happens to those who think they can be made right with God by their own good efforts?

Read Proverbs 16:18 for some insight into this practice.

In God's Word we are provided with a trilogy of New Testament books that in many ways expand, explain, and expound upon Habakkuk 2:4. We can see this in:

- Romans 1:15-17 (the just shall live by faith)

- Galatians 1:6-9; 3:1-3, 11 (the just shall live by faith)

- Hebrews 10:38 (the just shall live by faith)

Reread: Galatians 3:12

Also read: Leviticus 18:5 and James 2:10

Why does combining the Law with faith or simply obeying a list of rules and faith not work?

Read: James 2:14-20

What happens when one has true faith or trust in Jesus Christ?

Is this somewhat paradoxical? Does one who has truly trusted Jesus Christ end up living a life that is in concert with the Spirit and intent of the Old Testament Law?

How do you see this playing out in your own life?

Reread: Galatians 3:13

The Greek word for *redeemed* or *rescued* in this verse means to "buy out of slavery." How does this understanding of the Greek impact your understanding of this verse?

Read 1 Peter 3:18 for a greater understanding of this.

The manner of Jesus' death was a great obstacle for the Jews (See Deuteronomy 21:22-23). This was, however, completely turned around when they realized that the death He suffered and the curse He bore was for them (See Isaiah 53).

How do you think, feel, and respond when you realize that the death He suffered and the curse He bore was also specifically and personally for you?

Reread the following verses:

Galatians 3:14

Galatians 3:2

Galatians 3:8

Galatians 4:5

In what way can both Jews and Gentiles experience God's promised blessing apart from works of the Law?

This is a reference to the promised blessing of justification apart from works of the Law available to *all who believe*. It is not to be confused with national or personal blessings. Getting these concepts confused and intertwined leads to problems in understanding the unique roles of Israel and the church, the overall plan of God and ultimately His plan for each one of us.

Application Question

How can you help new or younger believers, who have not yet established the sufficient biblical base they will eventually attain, come to a clear understanding of their position in Christ?

Close in Prayer

THE LAW, THE PROMISE, AND FAITH
GALATIANS 3:15-25

Opening Prayer

Group Warm-up Question

What is the oldest legal document you own?

Read: Galatians 3:15-25

Reread: Galatians 3:15

What are the primary characteristics of an irrevocable agreement?

In an interesting twist, some of the early Judaizers may well have agreed that Abraham was made right with God through faith, but tried to argue that the Law, when given later, changed the basis for being "saved" to a system of works. To refute this, Paul points out that a properly executed Roman covenant cannot be arbitrarily set aside or changed, which shows that the promises of God are immutable. As we see throughout the Scriptures and life, God always keeps His promises.

Reread: Galatians 3:16

Read: Genesis 12:1-3

Read: Matthew 1:1

Through whom were the promises to Abraham fulfilled?

The promises given to Abraham and his seed were fulfilled in Christ and in effect forever. The method of being put right with God through faith (justification) is therefore permanent and was not changed by the giving of the Law.

Read:

Genesis 12:7

Genesis 13:15

Genesis 24:7

Genesis 12:1-3

John 4:22

Genesis 17:3-4

Genesis 17:7

Genesis 17:13

Genesis 17:19

Leviticus 26:40-45

Deuteronomy 30:1-3

How do the promises given to the Jews as a people relate to the promises fulfilled in Christ?

You can see all of human history laid out in advance, albeit in abbreviated form, in these amazing passages from the Old Testament. When tied in with what we learn in the rest of Scripture as a whole, as well as what we see in history, the Word of God becomes even more awe-inspiring.

Reread: Galatians 3:17

Read: Exodus 12:40

How long after the promises to Abraham was the Law given?

Why could the agreement that God made with Abraham not be broken?

Reread: Galatians 3:18

What is the relationship between the inheritance, the Law, and the promise?

Reread: Galatians 3:19

Read: Acts 7:53

What was the purpose of the Law?

For how long was the Law put into effect?

If you were a Jew living during the Old Testament era, how would the Law and the rest of the Tanakh (Old Testament) have benefited you on a personal basis?

Reread: Galatians 3:19-20

What exactly does a mediator do?

In what types of circumstances might a mediator be required?

In what way did Moses serve as a mediator?

If the Law required a mediator, how was God's promise given to Abraham without a mediator?

According to the text, does this infer that the promise to Abraham was unilateral?

If this promise was unilateral and unchanging, what does it mean for:

- Jews?
- Both Jews and Gentiles?

Reread: Galatians 3:21-22

Why do you think God gave both the Law as well as the promise?

In what way was the Law inadequate in and of itself?

Reread: Galatians 3:22-23

Why was the Law necessary to pave the way for Jesus Christ?

Reread: Galatians 3:23-25

The Greek word for "guardian, tutor or schoolmaster" in Galatians 3:24, depending upon which translation one may be using, is *paidagogos*. This is somewhat difficult to render into English for us today since there is no exact parallel in our modern society. In a historical sense, the *paidagogos* (where we get our word *pedagogue*) with which Paul was familiar, was a slave to whom a son was committed from age six or seven to puberty. These slaves were severe disciplinarians and were charged with guarding the children from the evils of society and giving them moral training.

How does this understanding of the Greek further add to your understanding of the role and purpose of the Law?

How did the life, death, and resurrection of Jesus Christ change the role of the Law?

What freedom does faith in Christ provide?

Why did Paul go to such great lengths to explain God's Law and God's grace in his letter to the Galatians?

Why did the Holy Spirit find it necessary and important to expound upon the relationship between God's Law, His grace, and His promises in so many of the other books of the New Testament?

Does this have anything to do with the fact that almost all of the first believers were Jews?

Read:

Romans 3:9

Romans 3:23

Romans 8:3-4

Would it be possible to be put right with God by following the Law if one were able to keep it?

How is it that we are able to satisfy the just requirements of the Law?

Application Questions:

How has trusting Jesus Christ set you free from legalism on a personal basis?

How has God fulfilled His promises in your life?

How can you help an unbelieving friend understand that being a good, law-abiding person is not enough to make him or her right with God?

Close in Prayer

TRUE CHILDREN OF GOD
GALATIANS 3:26-4:7

Opening Prayer

Group Warm-up Questions

What might be some of the advantages of growing up in a neighborhood with different ethnic groups?

What might be some disadvantages?

Read: Galatians 3:26-4: 7

Reread: Galatians 3:26

What is the new "family status" of those who have trusted Jesus Christ?

Reread: Galatians 3:27

Read: 1 Corinthians 12:12-13

According to these verses, how are believers joined to Christ?

What does it mean that believers have "put on Christ, like putting on new clothes?"

In Roman society, when a youth came of age he was given a special toga. This toga admitted him to the full rights of the family and the state and it indicated to others that he was an adult son.

Understanding the culture into which these verses were introduced, what else do you understand about the meaning of "putting on Christ?"

Reread: Galatians 3:28

How does God cut across cultural and human distinctions in the family of faith?

Paul may have been addressing a prayer that some men prayed during this time period: "I thank God that Thou hast not made me a Gentile, a slave, or a woman."

Read: Colossians 3:11

Which distinctions are significant in the body of Christ so far as spiritual privilege and position are concerned?

These verses call us to realize the coequality of men and women as well as Jews and Gentiles in Christ. However, we must also realize that there are distinctions. Spiritual service is one of those areas (1 Corinthians 11:3, 1 Timothy 2:12).

Jews and Gentiles who are in Christ are coequals. That being said, we must also realize the unique differences God has given them regarding national promises as well as the role He has given to the believing Jewish remnant in contrast to the role of the church. The church has not supplanted Israel in the plan of God, nor has it become "the new Israel." To make such a statement reads something into the Scriptures that simply is not there (See Acts 15:16 and Amos 9:11-12).

Reread: Galatians 3:29

In what way were the Galatians, and in fact, any Gentile believers, heirs to the promise made to Abraham?

How are Jews heirs to the promise made to Abraham in a way that is the same as Gentiles?

How are Jews heirs to the promise made to Abraham in a way that is different from non-Jews?

Differences in culture and practice can create differences both vast and subtle as human beings relate to each other. Many times these differences, when not taken into account or fully understood, prevent people from having effective interactions.

What are some cultural or sub-cultural differences that you have observed in society that can be difficult to overcome? (This can even include the vocabulary and sentence structure used by different groups. It might also include the way in which spouses are treated.)

How can believers work to both respect and yet overcome cultural barriers as they represent Christ?

How must believers respond when the cultural barriers they must overcome clearly contradict the Word of God?

Reread: Galatians 4:1-2

In what way might those who live under the Law, or in accordance with merely a strict set of rules, be said to be immature?

Reread: Galatians 4:3

Before the Galatians became believers, how were they like slaves?

    The Galatians were pagan Gentiles prior to becoming believers. The Jews had the Law from the Tanakh (Old Testament).

What then did it mean to the Jews to have been slaves under the Law before they became believers?

What did it mean to the Galatians (non-Jews) to have been slaves?

Read: Colossians 2:20

In what way was the slavery that both the Jews and Gentiles experienced prior to becoming believers the same?

As we saw earlier, under Roman law, a child ceremonially donned a special toga, called the *toga virilis,* when his father formally acknowledged him as his son and heir. The child's father was in charge of determining the age at which this occurred. Minor children were not officially recognized as heirs until they were officially adopted as sons in this fashion.

What further insight do we gain when we understand this tradition in light of Galatians 4:1-3?

We should realize that this concept is much different than what one sees in the world today. How often have you heard it said that "everyone is a child of God?" However, the Word of God refutes this statement. Read the following verses and discuss this difference:

John 1:12

John 3:3

John 3:5-6

John 3:14-16

Reread: Galatians 4:4

As we contemplate human history, it is amazing to see just how God ordered events, setting the stage for the perfect time to send His Son. Let's consider a few of those events:

1. The Romans enforced a peace that made far-ranging communication and travel possible.

2. In addition to enforcing this peace, the Romans built a heretofore unrivaled system of roads that made communication and travel possible.

3. The Greek civilization created a language that was accepted as the *lingua franca* of the Roman Empire. (*The Encyclopedia Britannica* defines *lingua franca* as a "Language used for communication between two or more groups that have different native languages.")

4. The Greek language was more exacting and developed than any other and as such was uniquely able to better communicate the message of the Messiah and to tie this message into the whole of Scripture.

5. By this time, the Jews had proclaimed monotheism and the hope of and in the coming Messiah in the synagogues of the whole of the Mediterranean world.

As we read the Old Testament we also see that the time of Jesus' coming itself was precisely predicted by the prophet Daniel as part of the flow of human history (See Daniel 9: 24-27).

What other things can you think of that were in place at the right time, setting the stage for the first coming of Jesus Christ?

Reread: Galatians 4:4-5

How did the coming of Jesus perfectly satisfy the requirements of the Old Testament Law?

What great benefit mentioned in verse 5 do believers experience?

We see several important concepts alluded to in Galatians 4:4-5. Seeing these concepts corroborated elsewhere in God's Word helps us to see the perfect integration of the whole of Scripture as God's message system to us.

1. The eternal Sonship of Christ and His role.

    Read:

    1 John 4:9

    I John 4:10

    John 3:16

2. The virgin birth of the Jewish Messiah, Yeshua Ha-Maschiach, also known as Jesus Christ.

    Read:

    Isaiah 7:14

    Matthew 1:18

3. The relationship of Jesus Christ to the Law.

   Read:

   Matthew 5:17

   Galatians 3:13

   2 Corinthians 5:21

Reread: Galatians 4:6

Whom does God send into the lives of believers?

What is it significant about the fact that God's Spirit "enters the hearts of believers" in contrast to the hearts of those who are not believers?

What exactly does it mean that God's Spirit enters the hearts of believers?

The term *Abba* is the diminutive form of *av* (literally meaning "the father") used by small children in addressing their fathers. It is appropriately compared to the English usage of the word "Daddy." This familiar form indicates extreme trust and intimacy. Old Testament believers never fully realized this relationship with God as a father. They were servants. It was only after the resurrection of Jesus and Pentecost that the full meaning of becoming a child of God was realized. This method of addressing God as *Abba* was not used by believers until then.

Read: Mark 14:36

Reread: Galatians 4:6

Read: Romans 8:15

Why does God's Spirit entering into one's heart enable a person to address God as "Abba, Father?"

Reread: Galatians 4:7

Since the Galatians were no longer slaves, what were they?

Read: Romans 8:14-17

How does this relate to believers today?

While we can become children of God by trusting Jesus Christ, we must remember that there is still a distinction between the position of Christ as the Son of God and our position as children of God.

Read John 1:1-3 to see that Christ is still the Creator and we are created.

Read John 20:17 to see the differentiation between us as children of God and Jesus as the Son of God. Notice that He speaks of "My father" in comparison to "your father," and "My God" in comparison to "your God." There is still a positional difference.

Read Psalm 22:22 to see this spoken of in advance in the Old Testament.

We become His children through faith in His Son. When one becomes a child of God in the real and true sense, one also assumes a certain responsibility. One is taking upon oneself the very name of God as a member of His family when calling oneself a believer or a Christian.

Read the following verses and discuss how this concept of responsibility relates directly to us today:

Exodus 20:7

Deuteronomy 5:11

Romans 2:24

1 Timothy 6:1

Application Questions:

As a child of God, do you behave more like a slave to the Law or your old nature, or more like an heir?

What can you do to behave more like a true child of God?

Close in Prayer

STAYING ON THE ROAD
OF TRUTH
GALATIANS 4:8-20

Opening Prayer

Group Warm-up Question

When, how, and why have you become estranged from a former friend?

Read: Galatians 4:8-20

Reread: Galatians 4:8

Before they became believers, to what were the Galatians enslaved?

Read: Acts 14:8-13

Lystra was a town in the region of Galatia, which is now part of present day Turkey.

What insight does this event give you into the difficulty some of the people of the region had with false gods?

Reread: Galatians 4:9

After the Galatians knew God, how did they begin to go back to some of the "weak and useless spiritual powers of this world?"

Why do you think they began to do this?

What are some of the "weak and useless principles" by which non-believers live their lives today?

Why do you think some people become believers and then return to their former destructive habits?

Reread: Galatians 4:10

As we mentioned earlier, the Judaizers believed that in order to be put right with God one first had to convert to Judaism. After all, from their point of view, everything that was good and came from God, including the Messiah, came through Judaism. Under their influence, some Galatians had started to observe the Mosaic calendar. These special days are the 70 HaMoyadim, or "the appointed times," and include weekly Sabbaths, and seasonal festivals such as Passover, Pentecost, Tabernacles, etc.

There is obviously great merit in observing these special times. However, doing so does not make one right before God (justification) nor does such observance in and of itself transform one into the person God desires him or her to be (sanctification).

Read: Colossians 2:16-17

To what do all of these appointed times point?

Read: Matthew 11:28

Do you think the Sabbath rest points to resting in Jesus Christ in addition to its obvious physiological, psychological, emotional, and spiritual benefits? Why?

Read 1 Corinthians 5:7-8 for a brief statement about how Christ has become our "Passover lamb" (NLT, NIV84).

Read: John 12:23-24 for greater insight into the fulfillment of the Feast of First Fruits.

Reread: Galatians 4:11

What was Paul's concern for the Galatians?

Why did he express his concern as he did?

    The Greek word used for Paul's efforts is *kekopiaka* which means laboring to exhaustion. He seems to be saying, "I have labored to the point of exhaustion."

What additional understanding or insight might we gain from this analysis of the original language?

The Greek word for "nothing" or "in vain" is *eijkh*. This same word is found in Galatians 3:4.)

How might you tie Galatians 4:11 and Galatians 3:4 and their usage of *eijkh* together?

Reread: Galatians 4:12-14

How did the Galatians treat Paul when he first came to them?

Read: 2 Corinthians 12:9

How did God use Paul's weakness and infirmity?

How can God use our weaknesses and infirmities?

Read: 1 Corinthians 9:20-21

How does this passage explain the way in which Paul lived both among the Jews as well as among the Gentiles?

Why was this so effective?

How might we apply these principles in our lives?

Why then was it so ironic that the Gentiles were putting themselves under the Law *after* they became believers?

Reread: Galatians 4:15-16

How did the Galatians' attitude toward Paul change?

Why was this change so heartrending for Paul?

Read: Proverbs 27:6

How does this principle relate to the way Paul was dealing with the Galatians in this situation?

Reread: Galatians 4:17

What seems to have been the motivation of the false teachers confronting the Galatians?

Were some of these people seeking God, but misled or were they more interested in aggrandizing themselves?

Does it seem correct to say that Paul came to the Galatians in self-denying service and love and the legalists came seeking to extend their own influence?

What notes of caution for our own lives might we draw from what was happening with Paul, the legalists, and the Galatians? List as many as you can.

1.

2.

3.

4.

5.

6.

7.

Reread: Galatians 4:18-19

In verse 19 Paul addressed the Galatians as his dear children (*tekna mou* in the Greek). This is the only place Paul uses this phrase in all of his writings. As the text indicates, Paul is thereby comparing himself to a mother in the throes of birth pains.

What is the significance of Paul using a term indicating such deep pain and anguish in this, and only this situation in his writings?

In the second half of verse 19, Paul makes a significant change of metaphors. What change does he make?

Why is this so important?

Read: Galatians 2:20 and Romans 12:2

How do these verses tie into what Paul so fervently wanted to see in the lives of the Galatians?

Reread: Galatians 4:20

Why did Paul want to be with the Galatians "right now?"

Why was this situation so perplexing and difficult for Paul?

Application Question

How can we show concern and love for believers who seem to have gotten off the path of God's truth?

Close in Prayer

FREEDOM IN CHRIST
GALATIANS 4:21-31

Opening Prayer

Group Warm-up Question

If you had siblings as you grew up, how were you and they treated differently in your family? If you did not have siblings, what have you observed in other families?

Read: Galatians 4:21-31

Reread: Galatians 4:21

Why did Paul ask the Galatians if they knew what the Law actually says? (Remember, he was writing to Gentiles.)

Do you think the Galatians would have been as attracted to keeping the Old Testament Law from the outset if they realized that it incorporates 613 separate rules?

Reread: Galatians 4:22

How did Paul's use of two of Abraham's sons as examples lend itself to helping the Galatians understand what the Holy Spirit was trying to get across to them?

Reread: Galatians 4:23

What was the most important difference in the way these two sons were conceived?

What is the significance of this difference?

Reread: Galatians 4:24-25

How did Hagar represent the covenant at Mt. Sinai?

Reread: Galatians 4:26-28

How did Sarah represent the heavenly Jerusalem and the new covenant in Jesus Christ?

Read Isaiah 54:1

How did Paul apply this ancient prophecy?

Read Hosea 12:10 and 1 Corinthians 10:11.

How did God use examples such as the one Paul is employing in this instance?

The use of Hagar and Sarah as illustrations to show the difference between human efforts to realize God's promises (Hagar) in contrast to God's own action to do so (Sarah) is an effective tool. This is an allegory and it is not only apparent on the surface, but also in the context of its usage as well as the presentation by the author.

This is entirely different from human efforts to utilize "allegorical interpretation," which has unfortunately been followed by Origen, Augustine, and many others through the ages right down to the present day. The problem with "allegorical interpretation" is that it elevates the fanciful opinions and thoughts of certain theologians above the Scriptures themselves. Historical facts and realities are relegated to the back seat as the opinions of self-important and proudly learned human beings come to the fore as they search for the hidden meanings that they wish to impute to God's Word. We must avoid this error at all costs. (For helpful information on allegorical interpretation and how to avoid such error, please see Appendix 1.)

It is our desire and goal to learn what God's Word says to us through the power of the Holy Spirit and to apply it to our lives with joy, prayer, thanksgiving, and power (1 Thessalonians 5:16-22).

Reread: Galatians 4:25-26

What do you make of the two contrasting references to Jerusalem in these verses?

It may be helpful to realize that in the first century, the city of Jerusalem was enslaved to both Rome and the Law. It was the center of the legalistic Jewish religion at that time. It was precisely because they "knew not the time of their visitation," that the Jews were driven out of Jerusalem. Read the following verses to see this, making sure to have at least one reader share from the King James Version of the Bible:

Matthew 27:25

John 19:15

Luke 19:44

In Galatians 4:25-27 we also see several direct comparisons either illustrated or alluded to. We see:

- Two women—Hagar and Sarah

- Two sons—Ishmael and Isaac

- Two covenants—Law and grace

- Two mountains—Sinai and Cavalry

- Two cities—earthly and heavenly Jerusalem

In the following verses we also learn more about this heavenly Jerusalem. You can see from the context that this is a real place, not an allegorical concept developed by those who have difficulty accepting the truth of God's Word.

Hebrews 12:22

Hebrews 11:10

Philippians 3:20

Revelation 21:2

Are you a citizen of heaven? How do you know?

Is this the citizenship that prioritizes your life? How does your life reflect your priorities?

Reread: Galatians 4:27

A final word about this verse; here we see Paul utilizing the prophecy from Isaiah 54:1 and relating it to Sarah. (Paul quotes this verse and applies it directly to the issue at hand in Galatians. However, as with many other portions of Scripture, Isaiah 54: 1 has both a contemporary application as well as a prophetic element.) This prophecy predicts the changing fortunes of Israel when seen in the context of Scripture as a whole. We see:

- The barrenness of Israel during the Diaspora (the dispersion of the Jewish population throughout the world) when she rejected her Messiah in Hosea 1 and Hosea 2. (Especially Hosea 1: 10-11)
- Their blindness in Luke 19:44
- The continuation of their blindness until the full number of Gentiles comes to trust in Jesus Christ in Romans 11:25

Reread: Galatians 4:28

How were the Galatians like Isaac?

Read the following verses and discuss what Paul meant by what he said in Galatians 4:28.

John 3:3

John 3:5

Galatians 3:9

Galatians 3:22

Galatians 3:29

John 1:17

Reread: Galatians 4:29

How were the Judaizers like Ishmael?

The early believers were, almost to a person, Jewish. Jesus Christ came as the Jewish Messiah, Yeshua Ha-Maschiach. God used the Jews to bring His Word to the world, both in the Old and New Testament. It was almost to be expected that this might lead to some confusion in the minds of religiously and rule-oriented Jews, even after they had been set free in Christ.

Read: Acts 15:4-11

How did Peter, a Jew from birth, respond to the Judaizers?

Read: Acts 15:13-21

How did James, a Jew from birth, respond to the Judaizers?

Read: Acts 15:22-31

What was the result of the way Peter and James responded to the legalists?

Reread: Galatians 4:30-31

Based upon Scripture and the illustration he used, how did Paul expect the Galatians to deal with the legalists?

Why do believers sometimes try to impose extra-biblical standards on one another?

How should you respond to people who try to impose their own standards on you?

The Galatians as well as other believers have already successfully dealt with the question; "Is there life after death?" However, some would say that in this passage we can see their struggle with the question; "Is there life after birth (the second birth)?"

How does this second question tie in with our discussion of legalism and freedom?

Read: 1 Corinthians 15:12-19.

If there were to be no life after birth for a believer (both now and beyond), how attractive would it be?

Application Questions:

What can you do to be sure you do not unfairly impose your personal standards on others?

What can you do to be sure that the standards to which you adhere and encourage others to follow are the same as God's standards?

Close in Prayer

Insight for Us as We Relate to Our Jewish Friends

Like many of the Gentiles we have read about, some of our Jewish friends have also had trouble putting together some of the concepts from the Tanakh (Old Testament) with those presented in what we call the New Testament. In reality, as we have come to discover, these documents and concepts fit together like a hand in a glove.

The Old Testament is not complete or able to be fully understood and appreciated without the New. And conversely, the New Testament must be viewed and understood in the context of the Old if we are to realize its full power and relevance.

- When we have Jewish friends who are willing to engage in thought, discussion, and honest inquiry into this matter, it is often helpful to suggest that they read the following excerpts from the Judeo-Christian scriptures. As they read these passages, we might suggest that they pray about what they are reading and ask that God show them His truth. They will be surprised at what the Holy Spirit reveals.

- Isaiah 53

- Psalm 22

- Psalm 69

- Zechariah 12-14

- The book of Hebrews

- The gospel of Matthew

FIGHT TO STAY FREE
GALATIANS 5:1-15

Opening Prayer

Group Warm-up Question

Do you prefer group or individual sports? Why?

Read: Galatians 5:1-15

Reread: Galatians 5:1

What challenge did Paul present to the Galatians?

Why did he have to put this challenge before them?

Read:

Galatians 3:24

Galatians 4:1-4

What role did the Law play before the sacrifice of Jesus Christ?

Read:

Romans 8:1-4

Galatians 4:5-7

How did Jesus Christ Himself satisfy the just requirement of the Law?

What role does the Holy Spirit, the "life-giving Spirit" (NLT), play in making this a reality in the lives of believers?

How does the inner discipline with which one can be enabled by the Holy Spirit contrast with the external legalism that enslaves those who try to be made right with God by following the Law?

Read:

Leviticus 26:13

Lamentations 1:14

How is trying to be put right with God by obeying the Law like a yoke of slavery?

Read: Matthew 11:28-30

How might one contrast the yoke of Christ with the yoke of the Law?

If the yoke of Christ is light and easy, why do believers sometimes face difficult and dire circumstances?

How might the yoke of Christ help believers face the trials they encounter?

Reread: Galatians 5:2

What warning did Paul deliver to the Galatians in this verse?

Reread: Galatians 5:3

How would turning to the Law obligate the Galatians?

Reread: Galatians 5:4

What is the severe consequence of seeking to be put right with God by obeying the Law?

What happens in the lives of people who try to be put right with God by obeying a list of rules and regulations?

As we see from these Scriptures, if we attempt to be put right with God by obeying the Law or a set of rules that seem good to us, we will be trying to pay a debt we cannot possibly satisfy. Conversely, if one trusts in Christ to be made right with God, that person actually becomes spiritually rich.

Read the following verses and list some of the ways in which one becomes spiritually rich when he or she follows Christ:

Ephesians 1:17

Ephesians 1:18

Philippians 4:19

Romans 11:33

Ephesians 3:8

Colossians 2:3

Colossians 2:10

Reread: Galatians 5:5

How did Paul contrast legalists and true believers?

How should believers respond to God knowing that we have this great promise?

Reread: Galatians 5:6

How did Paul characterize the significance of circumcision for a true believer?

Of what value then is circumcision?

How did God use both the symbolic and medical value of circumcision in His Word?

According to Galatians 5:6, what really matters?

Reread: Galatians 5:7

What had happened to the Galatians since becoming believers?

A literal translation from the original language would be: "You were running well. Who cut in on you so that you stopped obeying the truth?" How does this understanding help us better grasp what Paul was saying about the Galatians being influenced or pushed to change their focus and direction?

Reread: Galatians 5:8

To what does God call us?

How do some people abuse their freedom in Christ?

Reread: Galatians 5:9

Also Read:

Galatians 3:1

Galatians 1:6-9

Galatians 4:9

How had false teaching infected and impacted the Galatians?

How could it be that only one person going awry caused such a problem?

How can we guard against this today? Read Acts 17:11 as you construct your answer.

Is there a point at which someone who is leading others astray must be confronted, and ultimately moved outside of fellowship? Read 1 Corinthians 5:2 to help you answer this question.

Reread: Galatians 5:10

Why was Paul optimistic about the Galatians?

What consequences should the person introducing false teaching to the Galatians expect?

Reread: Galatians 5:11

What, in addition to the sacrificial death of Jesus Christ, makes it possible to for us to be made right with God? (Yes, this is a trick question.)

What are some of the unnecessary rules and regulations some people try to impose on others, even in the cause of Christ?

Reread: Galatians 5:12

How upset does it appear that Paul was with the Judaizers?

Why do you think this upset and apparently angered him so deeply?

What did he suggest that the Judaizers do?

How did this type of anger and response achieve the purpose of God?

Read:

Deuteronomy 27:26

Galatians 3:10

James 2:9-11

In what position did the Judaizers find themselves whether they realized it or not?

Warren Wiersbe tells a great story that dramatizes this situation. Imagine a motorist driving down the street and running a red light. This motorist is pulled over by a police officer who asks to see his driver's license. The driver immediately begins to defend himself by saying, "Officer, I know I ran that red light, but I've never robbed anyone. I've never cheated on my income tax. I've never murdered anyone."

The police officer simply smiles as he writes the ticket because he knows that no amount of obedience in the past can change the fact that the driver just ran the red light.

How might we apply this illustration to the concept of the Law of God?

Reread: Galatians 5:13

What kind of freedom were the Galatians called to?

Reread: Galatians 5:14

How did Paul sum up the whole Law?

How do you think this summary impacted the Judaizers and Pharisees of the time?

What happens to people when they abandon the grace of God for a set of rules?

Was this a new and unique summary of the Law that Paul came up with?

Read Luke 10:25-28 to see what Jesus Christ had to say about this.

Does this mean that there are no standards of conduct in the community of believers?

What is the ultimate guide for believers as they navigate life (2 Timothy 3:16-17)?

Reread: Galatians 5:15

What did Paul warn the Galatians against?

How might even a community of believers get involved with attacking and devouring one another?

What did Paul offer as the solution to this?

What challenge does this concept put before any group of believers?

The following quote is often cited in discussions of this nature: "In Essentials Unity, in Non-Essentials Liberty, in All Things Charity (Love)." Often attributed to great theologians such as Augustine, it comes from an otherwise undistinguished German Lutheran theologian of the early seventeenth century, Rupertus Meldenius. The phrase occurs in a tract he wrote about Christian unity (circa 1627) during the Thirty Years War (1618–1648), a bloody time in European history in which religious tensions played a significant role.

Do you think it is appropriate to apply this quote to our discussion today? Why or why not?

Application Questions:

As you run your race for Christ today, how can you free yourself from unnecessary rules and regulations that hinder your progress?

Whom among the people you know can you invite to join you in trusting Christ and "running the race of faith?"

Close in Prayer

FRUIT OF THE HOLY SPIRIT
GALATIANS 5:16-26

Opening Prayer

Group Warm-up Question

If you could change one personality trait in yourself, what would it be?

Read: Galatians 5:16-26

Reread: Galatians 5:16

What would have happened if the Galatians lived by the power of the Holy Spirit?

What would happen if we always lived by the power of the Holy Spirit?

What obstacle sometimes holds people back from living in the throes of this power?

Reread: Galatians 5:17

How were the Galatians impacted by the conflict between their old human nature and the Spirit?

How does this conflict impact you today?

Reread: Galatians 5:18

Also read:

Psalm 40:8

Hebrews 10:14-17

2 Corinthians 3

Why are believers not subject to the Law of Moses if they lead lives directed by the Holy Spirit?

If believers lead lives directed by the Holy Spirit, do they end up obeying the Law of Moses in some sense?

How do you see this playing out in actual experience?

Reread: Galatians 5:19-21

Also Read:

Mark 7:20-23

Romans 1:18-32

1 Timothy 1:9-11

2 Timothy 3:1-5

Paul has given us quite a list of sins in these passages. You will find some of the Greek words and definitions found in Galatians 5:19-21 below. This gives us a good idea of what the Holy Spirit is communicating to us:

- **Adultery,** or *moicheia* in the Greek, simply involves sexual relationships outside of marriage.
- **Fornication,** or *porneia* in the Greek, encompasses more than one might think. It includes illicit sexual intercourse, adultery, homosexuality, lesbianism, intercourse with animals, intercourse with relatives, and more. It is the root word from which emanates the modern term "pornography."
- **Uncleanness,** or *akatharsia* in the Greek, is a broad term referring to moral uncleanness in thought, word, and deed.

- **Lasciviousness,** or *aselgeia* in the Greek, connotes unbridled lust, wantonness, debauchery, insolence, and an open shameless brazen display of these evils.

- **Idolatry,** mentioned just after sexual sins, likely referred to the prostitution that was so often a part of pagan religions, as well as putting anything in the place of the living God.

- **Witchcraft** or **sorcery** comes from *pharmakeia* in the Greek. In pagan religions the worship of evil entities was accompanied by the use of drugs to create trances. Interestingly, we also see this device coming to the fore in Revelation 9:21 and Revelation 18:23.

- **Hatred** or **hostility** is *echthrai* in the Greek and used here in the plural form, indicating extreme ill will and enmity between groups.

- **Discord** or **quarreling** is a natural outcome of the hostility or hatred just mentioned.

- **Jealousy** or **emulations** is *zelos* in the Greek and refers to sinful and self-centered resentment for something someone else has. This often leads to envy.

- **Wrath** or **outbursts of Anger** is *thymoi* in the Greek. It refers to fits of rage and outbursts of temper. It often comes as a final eruption of smoldering jealousy.

- **Strife** or **selfish ambition** is *etitheiai* in the Greek and connotes a self-aggrandizing attitude which shows itself in working to get ahead at another's expense.

- **Seditions, dissensions** and **divisions** are *dichostasiai* and *haireseis* in the Greek and describe what happens when people quarrel over issues or personalities causing hurtful divisions.

- **Envy,** or *phthonoi* in the Greek, is an evil feeling and wrong desire to possess what belongs to someone else.

It is interesting to see the list capped off with two sins associated with alcohol:

- **Drunkenness,** or *methai* in the Greek, refers to excessive use of strong drink by individuals.
- **Wild parties,** or *komos* in the Greek, seems to refer to the drunken carousing commonly associated with such things as the worship of Bacchus, the god of wine.

How would you characterize the overall result of following one's human nature without listing specific activities, such as those above?

When a person follows his or her human or sinful nature, what results do we see relating to sex?

What results do we see relating to their religious activities?

How does this manifest itself in relationships with other people?

How does this impact that person's effect upon society?

In what way is the list that Paul puts forth in these verses incomplete (read Titus 1:15 as you think about your answer)?

When people are following their sinful nature, why do they often excuse themselves by saying "it's just my human nature?"

How does it impact individuals, society at large, and in fact the body of believers when someone excuses his or her actions by implying that the action in question is not his or her fault?

What warning does Paul provide at the end of Galatians 5:21?

What does Galatians 5:21 imply about the position of those engaging in the behaviors mentioned in relationship to God?

How might one relate Galatians 5: 19-21 with Proverbs 1:20-23?

Why do human beings sometimes think they can fool God?

What is the result and import of this attitude and the actions that follow?

Paul is solemnly warning the Galatians that those who habitually indulge in these sins will not inherit the future kingdom of God. He is not saying a person loses his or her salvation if he or she lapses into such a sin, but that a person who lives continually on such a level of moral corruption gives evidence of not being a child of God (Romans 6:15).

Read: Galatians 5:22-23

Also read: John 15:1-8

2 Corinthians 3:18

The fruit of the spirit is actually more involved than one might realize at first glance. To gain a greater appreciation of this, it might be helpful to break down Galatians 5:22-23 and look at it in the Greek. When we do this, we find that the fruit of the Spirit seems to be divided into three sub-categories:

1. Personal fruit: love, joy, peace
2. Outreaching fruit: patience, kindness, goodness
3. Fruit of general conduct: faithfulness, humility and self-control

Personal Fruit

1. **Love**, or *agape* in the Greek, is a divine love. It is sacrificial and seeks the good of the ones who are loved. This is the love God has for us and that resulted in Jesus Christ laying down His life for us individually and corporately. You can see the characteristics of this love in greater detail in 1

Corinthians 13:4-8 and learn more about it in 1 John 4:8, and John 3:16. This love can only be evidenced in one's life in a true sense through the power of the Holy Spirit.

This love is not the same as *eros*, the Greek word for sensual love, which incidentally is never used in the New Testament. Nor is it the same as *philia*, the Greek word for brotherly love, for which the United States city of Philadelphia, Pennsylvania is named and known.

2. **Joy**, or *chara* in the Greek, is a deep and abiding sense of inner rejoicing which was promised to those who abide in Christ (John 15:11). It does not depend on circumstances. It rests on God's sovereign control of all things (Romans 8:28). This joy actually imparts a person with strength (Nehemiah 8:10). One can see this in the life of Paul in Philippians 4:10-20. This joy is deeper and more complete than any human experience without the indwelling of the Holy Spirit.

3. **Peace**, or *eirene* in the Greek, is again a gift of Christ through the power of the Holy Spirit (John 14:27). It is an inner calmness and quietness even in the face of dire adverse circumstances. It is beyond the ability of humans to understand. It is impossible for one to experience this peace without the indwelling of the Holy Spirit (Philippians 4:7).

Outreaching Fruit

As in the case of the "personal fruit," none of the "outreaching fruit" can be effectively realized without the power of the Holy Spirit.

4. **Patience or longsuffering**, depending upon the translation you are using. In this case the Greek word used is *makrothymia*, which indicates forbearance under provocation or courageous endurance without quitting. It entertains no thoughts of retaliation even when wrongfully treated (See

2 Corinthians 6:6, Colossians 1:11, and Colossians 3:12). We should note that this does not negate the biblical concept and demand for justice and truth. All biblical truths work together in harmony when properly understood.

5. **Kindness**, or *chrestotes* in the Greek, is benevolence in action such as God demonstrated toward men. Since God is kind toward sinners, a believer ought to display the same virtue (Romans 2:4, Ephesians 2:7, 2 Corinthians 6:6, and Colossians 3:12).

6. **Goodness**, or *agathoisynei* in the Greek, is an uprightness of soul that results in reaching out to others and doing good to them even when it is not deserved.

Fruit of Conduct and Character

7. **Faithfulness**, or *pistis* in the Greek, is the quality which renders a person trustworthy or reliable (See Luke 16:10-12). Like a good United States Marine, whose motto is *Semper Fi* (always faithful, in Latin), a believer is to always be faithful.

8. **Humility**, or *prautes* in the Greek, marks a person who is faithful to God's Word and is considerate of others when discipline is needed. In earlier English usage this was often translated "meekness," which nowadays infers weakness. Nothing could be further from the truth. This quality is properly understood as power under control. The power comes from and is under the control of the Holy Spirit. There is no weakness here, just effective application of God's Word with the right attitude (See James 1:21, Galatians 6:1, 2 Timothy 2: 25, 1 Corinthians 4: 21, Ephesians 4:2, Colossians 3:12, 1 Peter 3:15-16).

9. **Self-Control,** or *enkrateia* in the Greek, denotes self-mastery and relates primarily to curbing the impulses of one's sinful human nature described in Galatians 5:19-21. This noun is used only here and in Acts 24:25 as well as 2 Peter 1:5-7 in the New Testament. Again we must note that this appropriate and powerful self-mastery or self-control comes only through the indwelling of the Holy Spirit.

What happens to a believer as a result of following the leading of the Holy Spirit in his or her life?

Is this an immediate event, a gradual occurrence, or in some strange way, both?

Can the Holy Spirit impact a believer in every area of his or her life? How so?

Special Assignment:

Memorize Galatians 5:22-23.

How might memorizing these verses help believers as they live their lives for God?

How might it help a believer if he or she were to recall these verses during their prayers?

In what other ways can a believer cultivate the character qualities brought about by the Holy Spirit?

Read: John 3:5-6

How does this tie in with what we have read so far about the fruit of the Spirit?

Reread: Galatians 5:24-25

Also Read:

Galatians 2:20

Romans 6:1-6

Colossians 2:11

Colossians 3:9

What has happened to the sinful nature of those who belong to Christ?

Does this mean that the sinful nature is gone? Please explain.

Does the fact that Paul encouraged the Galatians to follow the leading of the Holy Spirit when the Holy Spirit was already operant in their lives imply that they had a choice in the matter? (Read 1 Thessalonians 5:19 for corroboration.)

Do we have this same choice?

What do we need to do to access and utilize the power of the Holy Spirit in our daily lives?

In summary of Galatians 5:24-25, we might say our old nature must be overcome by:

1. Walking in the Spirit (Galatians 5:16)

2. Being led by the Spirit (Galatians 5:18)

3. Living in the Spirit (Galatians 5:25)

Believers have been regenerated and as such have available the divine enablement of the Holy Spirit (John 3:5-6 and Galatians 6:15-16).

Reread: Galatians 5:26

What warning did Paul give the Galatians in this verse?

This warning is placed in direct proximity to the fruit of the Spirit. Does this mean that engaging in these activities is both an act of the will as well as the result of not following the leading of the Spirit?

Does this also mean that engaging in these activities also prevents the power of the Holy Spirit from having reign in our lives?

How can we prevent this vicious snowball effect from impinging upon our lives?

Read: Titus 2:11-13

How does this relate to the warning we find in Galatians 5:26 and point us in the right direction?

Application Questions:

What can you do to nurture the growth of a Spirit-filled character in your life?

How can you, while accessing the power of the Holy Spirit, get rid of the things in your life that might be holding you back from being the man or woman God intends you to be?

Close in Prayer

WEEK 12

DOING GOOD TO EVERYONE
GALATIANS 6:1-10

Opening Prayer

Group Warm-up Question

How easily do you share your time and skill with others?

Having just reviewed the fruit of the Spirit in the previous chapter, the Holy Spirit now directs our attention to some specific and practical applications and uses of this fruit. In the verses we will consider today, Paul targets four specific areas. As we noted in the previous session, these things can only be done properly when one is doing so in the power of the Holy Spirit. The activities discussed go far beyond humanitarian actions; they are appropriately defined and practiced only when the spiritual dimension is satisfied by the indwelling of the Holy Spirit. These targeted areas of life include:

1. How we respond to believers who have fallen into some sort of sinful behavior.

2. How we relate to believers who are struggling with some sort of burden or difficulty.

3. How we support and relate to those in positions of teaching, leadership, and pastoral roles.

4. How we interact with all people, whether or not they are believers.

Read: Galatians 6:1-10

Reread: Galatians 6:1

How did Paul say we should respond when we see a believer overtaken by some sin?

What note of caution does God give us when we are engaged in helping someone who has had such a difficulty?

Read:

John 8:3-5

Acts 21:27-31

Galatians 5:15

How did the legalists of the first century respond when they thought someone was caught in some sort of wrongdoing?

Do people act this way today, sometimes even in religious organizations?

There is an unfortunate saying among some denominations that goes: "Christians kill their wounded." How does this contrast with what we read in Galatians 6:1?

Read:

1 Corinthians 2:15

Galatians 5:16

Hebrews 5:13-14

Who in the family of faith might be in a position to recognize when someone needs the help referenced in Galatians 6:1?

Reread: Galatians 6:1

In this verse we see reference made to setting someone back on the right path. The Greek word involved in this is *katartizo*. This word is used in secular Greek for the mending of bones. We also see it used in the New Testament in reference to the mending of nets.

How does this understanding of the Greek help us understand what God is trying to get through to us in this verse?

Read: John 8:7-11

How did Jesus Christ respond to someone caught in sin?

Read: 1 Corinthians 10:13

What promise do we have from our loving heavenly Father when we are faced with temptation?

Reread: Galatians 6:2

The Greek word used for burdens implies a very heavy burden or weight. How are we to respond to another believer who is burdened, and especially to one living under a very heavy burden?

Reread: Galatians 6:2

Also Read:

Galatians 5:14

John 13:34

What does it mean when it says "obey or fulfill the law of Christ?"

Reread: Galatians 6:3-4

Also read: Romans 12:3

How are we to think of ourselves?

How are we to avoid self-deception?

In the Greek, everyone is told to test *(dokimazo)* his or her own actions. This implies that instead of comparing oneself with others, one is to step back and take an objective look at his or her own accomplishments, life, and actions.

Read: 1 Peter 1:5-7

What is the ultimate result of our testing?

Reread: Galatians 6:5

How is carrying our own weight different from bearing the burdens of others?

How do these concepts work together?

The Greek word used for burdens in Galatians 6:5 is different than the word used in Galatians 6:2. The word used in Galatians 6:2 implies a crushing load or burden so heavy it could not be carried without help. Conversely, the word used for burden in Galatians 6:5 is *phortion*, which designates the pack normally carried by a marching soldier.

Read: Matthew 11:30

Does it appear that every believer is essentially assigned a burden or pack to carry as a soldier in the spiritual and cultural battle in which we are all engaged? How would you put this in your own words?

Larry Norman, the father of Christian rock music, didn't want to have a fan club, though some of his fans thought it was a good idea. Instead, he agreed to be a part of what he called "The Solid Rock Army" in which he and every other believer is called to serve.

What do you think of this concept?

Read:

Romans 15:1-2

John 3:16-17

Romans 12:6-8

What further insights do these verses give us about doing all of the following at the same time?

- Fulfilling our responsibility to carry our own weight
- Helping to bear the heavy burdens of other believers
- Being willing to accept help if and when our burden gets too heavy

What are some of the times in life when a believer might find he or she needs help with his or her burden from other members of what Larry Norman called The Solid Rock Army?

Have there been times in your life when you needed help with a burden that was heavy to bear? What happened?

Reread: Galatians 6:6

Read: 1 Corinthians 9:7-14

What should we share with those who serve as pastors and teachers?

What, beyond financial support, should we be sharing with those serving in these roles?

Reread: Galatians 6:7-8

How do you see these verses relating to our interaction with our leaders and teachers?

While these verses have some relationship to one's interaction with leaders and teachers as they flow from the preceding verses, they also go further. Read the following verses and comment on how the concepts in Galatians 6:7-8 fit with the same topic other places in God's Word:

Hosea 8:7

Job 4:8

Matthew 7:16

Matthew 7:17

Proverbs 1:24-33

Reread: Galatians 6:9

Do you see this as part of one's duty as a "soldier in God's army"?

Is this also a privilege? How so?

Reread: Galatians 6:10

Also read:

1 Timothy 5:8

Romans 12:9-10

Romans 12:17-21

How would you summarize the social responsibility of believers as alluded to in these verses?

Why are believers instructed to take care of their own families and fellow believers first?

How does God use the love between believers to communicate His message to the world?

Application Question

How can you help a fellow believer in your sphere of influence this week with a particularly heavy burden?

Close in Prayer

WHAT REALLY MATTERS

GALATIANS 6:11-18

Opening Prayer

Group Warm-up Question

What personal or family traditions are important to you?

Read: Galatians 6:11-18

Reread: Galatians 6:11

In considering Galatians 6:11, we should realize that it was Paul's custom to sign his letters in his own handwriting in order to authenticate them (See 2 Thessalonians 3:17-18). In this letter, however, and in this letter alone, Paul seems to have written the entire closing paragraph in his own hand in extremely large letters.

Why do you think Paul completed the letter this way and what was the Holy Spirit trying to accomplish by being sure that readers knew about it?

Could it be that the message being communicated in this last paragraph are so important that the Holy Spirit wants to be sure that we "stand up and take notice"?

Reread: Galatians 6:12-13

Why did the legalists want people to be circumcised?

In what way were the legalists hypocritical?

What did the legalists boast about?

The Judaizers or legalists described in these two verses have four negative characteristics that we are to avoid.

1. They are braggarts about their own works.

2. They have compromised to escape persecution.

3. They are great persuaders for the accolades they will receive, and not because of a primary desire to have others experience a new life through Christ.

4. They are hypocrites.

Reread: Galatians 6:14

What did Paul want to boast about?

What did Paul mean when he said he wanted to "boast of the cross of Christ?"

What was the extreme difference in the motivation and focus between Paul and the Judaizers?

Throughout the letter to the Galatians, Paul keeps drawing the readers back to the cross of Christ, His sacrifice, and the freedom that has been purchased for us by His sacrifice. Read the following verses that the Holy Spirit has strategically placed in this letter to see this occurring. As you read each verse, write down the specific and definitive points that are being made.

- Galatians 2:20-21
- Galatians 3:13
- Galatians 4:5
- Galatians 5:11
- Galatians 5:24
- Galatians 6:12

Upon examining the text of this letter, we find that Jesus Christ is mentioned at least forty-five times. This means that about one-third of the verses contain direct references to Him. What do you think God is trying to get across to us by doing this?

How does this tie into the way in which we are continually reminded of the cross of Christ and what it means?

Read: Philippians 3:4-6

If a person could make him or herself right with God through his or her own effort, how would Paul have fared compared to most other people?

Read:

Galatians 6:15

2 Corinthians 5:17

Romans 5:17

John 13:34-35

What important truths does the Holy Spirit hammer home to us in these verses?

Some people say that in many ways, Galatians 6:15 sums up the whole of the book of Galatians. What are your thoughts about such a statement?

Reread: Galatians 6:16

Be sure to read this in the NLT as well as the KJV.

This is an interesting verse. It incorporates references to two distinct groups who are recipients of the same blessing. The first group is the Gentile believers to whom most of the letter is addressed. The second group, translated the "Israel of God" in the KJV, refers to believing Jews.

We can see these two separate and distinct groups referenced earlier in this letter in Galatians 2:7-9. I mention this here only to avoid the confusion that creeps into one's understanding if upon a cursory reading of Galatians 6:16 in the KJV, one assumes that somehow the church has replaced Israel in the plan of God or that the two are one and the same. Such an assumption would also run counter to these topics as revealed in the whole of Scripture. The church and Israel have distinct functions and destinies. In some ways, there are similarities, but blurring the distinctions makes it difficult to clearly see the plan of God as delineated in His Word.

That is probably all we need to say about this concept in our study. Those who care to understand this with all of the attendant intricacies may want to read *Israelology: The Missing Link in Systematic Theology* by Arnold Fruchtenbaum. This intensely scholarly work was published by Ariel Minsitries Press of Tustin, California in 1993 and runs to 1,000 pages.

Read Galatians 6:16 in the NLT again.

Here we see the translators correctly getting across an important principle that relates to both believing Jews and believing Gentiles alike. Having said all of this, how would you put Galatians 6:16 in your own words?

Reread: Galatians 6:17

It almost seems Paul is saying he doesn't want to be bothered with this malarkey about the Judaizers again. He wants believers to press forward in their lives as believers and leave this pointless and destructive controversy behind. What do you think?

Do people today sometimes fall into the trap of endlessly concentrating and fretting about something that should be clearly defined and put to rest in their thinking?

Read: Hebrews 5:11-6: 3

How does it impact people when they do not go beyond the basics of the faith?

In Galatians 6:17, Paul also speaks of marks upon his body. These marks are referred to as *stigmata* in Greek and are signs of ownership, such as one might brand onto slaves or cattle.

Read the following verses to learn more about the scars on Paul's body that showed he belonged to Jesus Christ:

1 Corinthians 4:11

2 Corinthians 4:10-11

2 Corinthians 6:5

2 Corinthians 6:9

2 Corinthians 11:24-25

What does the fact that Paul bore these marks mean to you?

Warren Wiersbe says we should "beware of that religious leader who lives in his ivory tower and knows nothing of battling against the world, the flesh, and the devil and has no 'marks' to show for his obedience to Christ. Paul was no armchair general; he was out in the front lines, waging war against sin and taking his share of suffering."

Dr. Ron Moore says that in America most believers have never really suffered for their faith. The most suffering many have experienced has been to "endure" some negative comments in a discussion at Starbucks. What do you think about what Ron has said?

What marks from suffering, physical or otherwise, show that you belong to Jesus Christ?

Read:

Galatians 6:18

Galatians 1:3

Paul closes this letter in a fashion that is similar to the way he began it. What do you make of this as well as what he said in both places?

Paul also closes this letter a little differently than his other epistles. In Galatians, he reminds the recipients of the letter of his love for them, calling them brothers and sisters. What do you make of this?

What is the Holy Spirit trying to get across to us by closing the letter in this manner?

How do other believers recognize your love for them?

Application Question

How can you evidence to the world this week that you are becoming a new creation as referenced in Galatians 6:15 and John 13:34-35? Be very specific and concrete in answering this question. "Fluff" answers, such as "I will be kind" should be developed. Exactly what will you do?

Assignment:

Memorize Galatians 6:15.

> It doesn't make any difference now whether we have been circumcised or not. What counts is whether we really have been changed into new and different people. (Gal. 6:15 NLT)

By memorizng this verse and taking it to heart we can be certain that the benefits of becoming a new creation in Christ inure to us.

Close in Prayer

APPENDIX 1

HOW TO AVOID ERROR

(Referenced in Week 9)
(Partially excerpted from *The Road to Holocaust* by Hal Lindsey)

1. The most important single principle in determining the true meaning of any doctrine of our faith is that we start with the clear statements of the Scriptures that specifically apply to it, and use those to interpret the parables, allegories, and obscure passages. This allows Scripture to interpret Scripture. The dominionists (and others seeking to bend Scripture to suit their purposes) frequently reverse this order, seeking to interpret the clear passages using obscure passages, parables, and allegories.

2. The second most important principle is to consistently interpret by the literal, grammatical, historical method. This means the following:

   • Each word should be interpreted in light of its normal, ordinary usage that was accepted in the times in which it was written.

   • Each sentence should be interpreted according to the rules of grammar and syntax normally accepted when the document was written.

- Each passage should also be interpreted in light of its historical and cultural environment.

Most false doctrines and heresy of church history can be traced to a failure to adhere to these principles. Church history is filled with examples of disasters and wrecked lives wrought by men failing to base their doctrine, faith, and practice upon these two principles.

The Reformation, more than anything else, was caused by an embracing of the literal, grammatical, and historical method of interpretation, and a discarding of the allegorical method. The allegorical system had veiled the church's understanding of many vital truths for nearly a thousand years.

Note 1: It is important to realize that this is how Jesus interpreted Scripture. He interpreted literally, grammatically, and recognized double reference in prophecy.

Note 2: It is likewise important that we view Scripture as a whole. Everything we read in God's Word is part of a cohesive, consistent, integrated message system. Every part of Scripture fits in perfectly with the whole of Scripture if we read, understand, and study it properly.

Note 3: Remember to appropriate the power of the Holy Spirit.

Read: Luke 11:11-12   Read: 1 Timothy 4:15-16

Read: Luke 24:49   Read: 2 Peter 2:1

Read: John 7:39   Read: Mark 13:22

Read: John 14:14-17, 26